Through the window of life

Neha N Kulkarni

BookLeaf
Publishing

India | USA | UK

Presentation by *BookLeaf Publishing*

Web: www.bookleafpub.com

E-mail: info@bookleafpub.com

ISBN: 9789360949099

First edition 2024

Contents

1. Introduction To My Poetry.   1
2. On Inspiration.   2
3. That Seller Old Man at Roadside.   3
4. Five Years With a School Friend.   5
5. A Savouring Bite Along the Way.   6
6. On Those Little Birds.   8
7. That Tainted Golden Necklace.   9
8. A Forlorn Old Lady.   10
9. That Rainy Summer Night.   12
10. That Coconut Seller.   13
11. Midnight Travel in a City.   14
12. That Morning Green View.   15
13. A Passenger In a Train.   16
14. The Flow of Gratitude.   18
15. Once On A Lonely Road.   19
16. The Half Grin.   23
17. On That Balcony.   26
18. The Magic Box.   27
19. Within A Park.   28
20. The Inner Craftsman.   29
21. The Beauty Show.   30
22. Moonlight Memory.   31

23. The First Rain.   32

24. The Wakeup Call.   34

25. An Open Heart.   35

26. The Yearly Budding.   36

27. The Humble School.   37

28. Among That Line.   38

29. The Home Coming.   39

30. Those Words in Light.   41

31. Song Of The Falling leaf.   42

32. To Waterfalls.   46

Introduction To My Poetry.

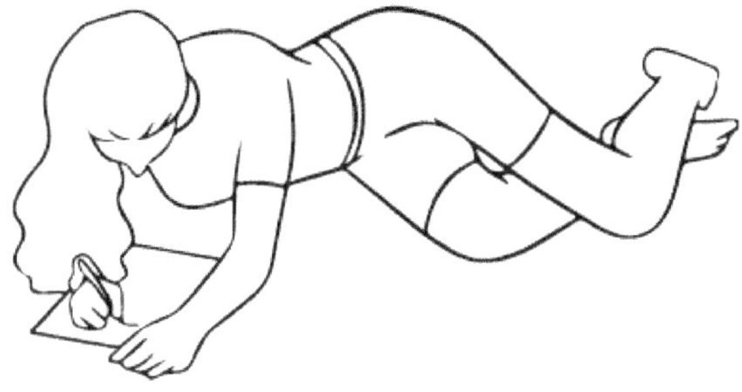

I may not build solely on moral stage.
What is that to eyes of a seeking child!
Nor would I erect those passions too wild.
But my mind would behold some scenes of age.
Then they shall vibrate on an empty page.
To print those emotions like deep, soft, mild.
When thoughts with letters will be reconciled,
They might try and touch my innermost sage.
Run with vigour, source of my words in heart.
Thou shall paint that I feel, from time to time.
Hold life with flavours sweet, salty, or tart.
Let all pass by as old, young or in prime.
As that Lord shapes my growth, so grows thy
art.
Yet let's preserve each other's hearts sometime.

On Inspiration.

Where did my thoughts fall as I saw a Rose?
On many metaphors and similes.
Lodged on Beauty, exploring outdoor glees.
Well, maybe on Nature's inspiring pose.
A faint mumble then from somewhere arose,
As I watched flowers thrilling in the breeze,
Which like me unknown to the ways of bees,
Danced oblivious to time's thorny dose.
The Beauty faded as their noise came near.
Then Nature had more than fine to reveal.
The sight from pleasant switched to loss and
fear.
To mind's eye or to those through whom I feel.
It was the life itself that Spake "Oh! Dear,
Your pen shall note many signs to appeal."

That Seller Old Man at Roadside.

How thine arms must have held strength in thy
Youth.
Yet retained energy though they shudder.
Those times what might have thine eyes spark
colour.
Though weak, they evinced me the hue of truth.
I know not, how thee crossed life in thy growth.
Can't guess either what has pressed thee thither.
My hands are frail to raise thy state hither,
Blood afresh they possess, skin a bit smooth.
How! Contrary does this game of life throw?

Since I sit in ride but thee must labor.
I may judge thee too to be friend or foe.
Placed I'm though to do thee not much favour,
From hence thine glimpse shall pass my mind
some glow,
And save faith in life if it did waver.

Five Years With a School Friend.

Were we not like two Roses in a Pot!
Not alive to the world around we dwelt.
Nor in acts Pomp did our soul Ever melt,
But boldly bore the weather cold and hot.
Smiled upon spikes with simple trust we got.
Bent never to hard winds of pain we dealt.
Together adorned all the joys we felt.
Ex guessing thee my wish and me thy thought.
Then soon that phase like some five seconds
passed.
Rough Destiny's hands arrived, we got plucked.
To décor halls varied we have been tossed.
Mind not what path for us life has installed.
Someday we may find our face beauty lost,
Our Love bides ever in love's Nectar soaked.

A Savouring Bite Along the Way.

Eyes flashed childishly on seeing him come.
Like Rain for thoughts minding a scorching heat,
He came lifting moods which were dim and dumb.
Parking the car, we all ran fast to meet.
A humble man, he was from some village.
With his cart crossing the path to our end.
That bell he rang at once gave us the nudge.
Those ice candies he sold made us descend.
"What a slice it is!" Exclaimed all damp mouth.

No costly Parlour holds this taste they told.
Cold things lacking that magic for days forth.
Whilst mere thirst for change made that act
unfold.
Ruffled views there sat behind a new bite.
Like daring smile on Trial, shrinks its height.

On Those Little Birds.

Once I saw the forms of true Serving Men.
Their eyes seldom blinking with tears on fate.
Toiling from the first ray till the dusk late,
Hardly hearts urging for palace or den.
Never failing to try each time again
Active now, not for time else they await.
Such stand in almighty eyes must be great,
Small birds they were but lived like in Heaven.
Palms of me are full, ample things I owned.
Been blessed by maker's huge grant of reason.
Yet mind hunted, for things fairer it moaned.
In neglect messed with nature and season.
By them, if learnt and to our lacks atoned.
May live gently, let live with least harm done.

That Tainted Golden Necklace.

There I was, where Men sat to get or give.
Weighty things on eyes were set for business.
While dealing, mind knows not to be reckless.
There a piece Shined bright as if to outlive.
But marked tiny spot made it defective.
Amid other pieces it sat helpless.
When place head also shoved it as useless,
As if to me that beauty gave its view.
"I Shall come again with new Shape and gleam.
This stain black on me if did never mend.
None can change my truth, I'm a Golden beam.
In all times a smile I would ever lend."
Days gone by, still it calls my truth to deem.
And the thought taught, left me and smile to
blend.

A Forlorn Old Lady.

Her strained eyes reflected Her owned Shelter.
That which hovers over all flavoured head.
Her wrinkled Cheeks showed age of that digs
dead.
Front of that ruin, she was a dweller.
Charity-drenched Mind on her life bitter.
Heart ached, on Her feeble hands baking bread.
Did she always live out in dark and dread?
Earth's daughter, did thee see days no better!
Lost in my thoughts depth and that place is null.

Harbours where she now, I know not a thing.
Many youths there walked with looks clear and
dull,
Fragile views broke their heart if missed
something.
She was old, but her form became model.
Her life weakened my arms, she lost nothing.

That Rainy Summer Night.

Who's knocking the door in such dark so loud!
Shaken in my deep slumber, I wondered.
Fancies such my mind at that time rendered,
As I heard violent footsteps of crowd.
Commanded by some Lord with his state
frowned.
On compromised rival lately faltered,
To keep peace. Such bangs got my sense
blundered,
But it was just a rash Thundering cloud.

That was the night after a heated day.
Sparkle of flash and sound lashed with the rain.
And like some wild beast plunging on its prey,
It rocked on the ears of a chosen lane,
Drifting into sleep I smiled at that play,
At times, Nature too finds our brain to reign.

That Coconut Seller.

Coco! CoCo! He yelled, dragging his load.
Shifting gaze from one door to another.
Calling all to come to him on that road.
Pleasing them as his sister or brother.
His eyes then fell on that house in that street.
Gave free straws to the wind which came flying,
Girl of three ran back with this special treat.
And he went daily with his eyes glinting.
That toddler lost wish as the game lost charm.
His grin went away, and his voice turned flat.
Few days his greetings spilled not fully warm.
But then, next day he smiled, forgetting that.
One closed door, he soon left against other.
As each turning page brings a new chapter.

Midnight Travel in a City.

On the way to my final destiny,
When man-made lights were glaring on those
few,
Out with them, who were on necessity.
I caught the song of the city brand new.
Quietly it came from out into mind,
Words it had were none on the tune of peace.
Then and there I left all concerns behind,
Hung on that city lullaby with ease.
Its hush fell like tongue-tasting sweet honey,
Besides those Rush of thoughts and jumbled
noise,
Ringing days appearing much too heavy,
As all dash to meet the ends they devise.
Then I reached, some words hit me of the song.
"That taste sense is thine not to me belong."

That Morning Green View.

Oft, doth me see this world with rays of dawn.
But nay, felt not its act on nature green.
So, firm they stood rooted as Sacred queen,
Of Divine love with Heart and Soul at loan.
Bathing their palms, each vein, and every bone,
In that Universal love song Serene.
Though time too for them is then, now and been,
They'll glory on their precious Golden Stone.
Lord! Bless me, I was drowned in that live
dream.
So Pious love was unveiled before me.
Touch of rising Sun through radiant stream,
Laid Pearl on each short, long grows of the lea.
Although time screened away that lovely scene,
Let the shine in me reside, doth I plea.

A Passenger In a Train.

Those mini feet jumping on the whistle.
The eager gaze resting out of window,
That blooming face with smiles in that hustle,
Pinched some lost reminiscence to follow.
Some long-missed friend like she got my heart
moved.

I with swift thoughts began watching her step.
Thorough I viewed yet it got nothing proved.
Her friends were not known, never were we met.
Features of her did seem so familiar,
Queries in heaps by her felt resounding.
Next to the eyes on screen or tones greyer,
Dear was her game, intriguing her finding.
Sleeping then, as child changed places with her.
Thus was I answered by dream in mirror.

The Flow of Gratitude.

As a piece of some vast knitting pattern,
Time seized me to fix some pretty design.
The circle was made, I came for my turn.
Birth dropped me among threads of my
bloodline.
New skill got into force as I'm growing.
Fresh yarns of life came adding to my tale.
Some stick with me, some come and are going.
Some with my joys, some soothing when I fail.
One tending sickness, one patting my back.
One smoothing pride, other on terms fairly.
Ever swelling the value of my track.
A gift to my beauty, called family.
Great king as the mind seeks through them
standing.
The worth of them just keeps on augmenting.

Once On A Lonely Road.

Once on a lonely Road,
I was walking carefree and all alone.
There came two voices on my back,
Calling my name: alas! I didn't like their tone.

As I turned, I saw two Policemen,
Rushing towards me with handcuffs in their
hands.
They tied my arms and drew me with them,
Pushing me finally inside a lonely little cellar.

I screamed for help, pleaded for release.
Tried the ways to run myself.
But they just stood calmly barring the way out,
Casting now and then curious glance upon my
struggles.

Some minutes went by without them shifting.
As I composed somewhat, their view came to
my notice.
Abruptly their uniform vanished, some casuals
they attired.
As if known me long they bestowed friendly
looks.

Being puzzled, I asked after their business.
On that query a smile extended on their faces,
Glancing at each other once then looking at me,
They gradually approached and stood on either
side.

"I'm named Introspection," said the one on my
right.
"I'm here to examine thy thoughts and mental
ability.
Behold my eyes and see a life within thee,
And note thyself what was thy advancement."

On those words a laughter I heard from my left.
Saying that he had better things, the other
grabbed attention.
He called himself Retrospection then disclosed
his intention.
For examination offered some precious past
events.

The laugh sprang from both after that.
My own choice was then opened for me.
Either together or else one after the other,
Informing thus, they stood statue-like moving in
the middle.

Then I reflected upon myself looking for his
meaning,
I toured in the past to consider his words.
Both travellers held a box of sweets for my
taking.
And released me from the ties as I was finished.

Gently taking my arms they brought me to the
door,
But before I stepped out, at once they spoke.
"Who amongst us was thy home?" They
enquired.
"Which between us defined thy persona?" They
asked.

I looked at them and laughed at my turn,
For neither of you accomplished me, I said.
As I'm that observant tree underneath which I
was sleeping,
And you both are just parts of my passing time.

Then I turned neither a tree nor a sleeping eye.
Sitting up, I felt as weary as if gone very far.

A smile absorbed my heart as I recalled events
with their impression.
As if fed sweets from those twins of mind, they
come and enchant some of my solitary
repose.

The Half Grin.

Some speech into my ears that day,
Ensured about the ugliness of the clouds.
Others then amusing on the other half,
Talked of the Beauty of the Sun.

Then few commented on the break they saw,
Brought by the covering over seething rays.
While some said the forbearing of the humid.
Before the air is cool as the rain concludes,
annoying can be its sport.

I in my mind took that half grin of the sky,
Allowed my best to join its fun.
But the hidden half-Sun with layers there about,
Brought some expression within me of my own.

The convergence of them plagued for some time,
Telling me about the confluence of life.
Equating enjoyment the Sun smiled in half,
Threatened by thick sheets of sorrows of mine.

The union of cheerfulness and pains clenching
the thoughts,
Life's two unstable stages I looked everywhere.
Unfelt really the pleasures ran so fast.

And hurts not only left injuries but some help for
improving me.

Betwixt them mind just playing the victim,
Life is like a drama being spun around.
Till my awareness attached there as real me,
The hunt for fun and bother of pain goes on.

But the thinking mind is a blessing in disguise.
Its inquisitive freedom like a child in pursuit of
the truth,
Went and watched the sky stretched inside the
Heart.
There the illusions depart, and reality moves in
front.

Then the picture up there had not much to
display.
But the natural Beauty of two of its members.
The Sun blazed peaceably from within, just
obscured.
The menacing clouds merely stood performing
their task.

But my temporary pleasures began ebbing away.
With hunt out in the world, some trail in me
awoke.
For burning restless thoughts, I longed for Sun's
tranquillity.

Ugly depressing moods look for the shower of
unending happiness.

Thereafter burst of spirit takes place as I go into
myself.
With Life emerging throughout in new light.
And the meditating in and out for refining of me
and mine,
Effects the confluence of me with true living as
the challenge.

But the eyes keen to see ahead of two shades in
life,
Moving through the tunnel into brilliant light
initiated,
Craving for more on that road as the torch of
that lonely going,
Has the broadness of life knocking the door with
that enterprise.

On That Balcony.

On my Gaze the window glided apart.
Waves and waves of life started to rush pass.
A fair it was, of ones within the mass.
A kid wailing there, here a youth dressed smart.
A group shopping in, a man to depart.
A boy on phone, a mother with her lass.
Birds flying up there, dog sprawling on grass.
Each manifesting some thought to impart.
And there I'm, on my balcony strolling,
Part of same picture yet feeling aloof.
Now digging past, then in future running.
But when in moment, I felt lives rolling,
Its Just Spirit was bare from down to roof.
Stunned I was with oneness midst the tuning.

The Magic Box.

"My wand makes world in this world," it said
once.
"Hold medicine for all thy weariness.
Matters not thy worries once through my trance,
The next light thee shall have thy readiness.
Things thee give me I can turn it pleasant,
Arranging them with fragrance of thy touch.
A space I create with things for thy rest,
People in this box are those thee miss much.
Thee may shout here and speak thy silent hurts.
I know to clear those clouds crossing thy face.
Witness I'm also of all thy efforts,
Lolling in my spell would fetch back thy pace.
I'm the thing thee name home," it revealed
when,
Saw place invoking peace that's caged within.

Within A Park.

Incensed then with many things utterly,
I was there inside a formed surrounding.
Thoughts of days with all their uncertainty,
Had mind Captive like in a maze rounding.
Fighting in, to wandering I retired.
But soon was taken in by a numbness.
Content to nothing, I called myself tired.
Looked around to escape my fruitlessness.
Light breeze there after brushing passed my hair,
Touch of cool grass below washing soles,
Draught coming with some healing to my care,
Lounging on bench I reached for simple grace.
Calm voice of Heart sent rhythm back to feet.
Rising then exposed sky as my limit.

The Inner Craftsman.

A while it was a bird stretching its wing.
Like dreams up to go beyond sky in flight.
Then there was a little boy out cycling,
Eager to catch the group behind the kite.
Like young wishes, few flowers sat in bloom,
An old man's stick to chide sitting beside.
Then hut was there like secret with closed room,
Comprising no door, no person to hide.
A Deity sat calmly around too.
Smiling down, blessing fingers pointing up.
A blue screen running all behind this move,
This craft of white cotton floated on top.
Above mind carved its riddles like magic,
I sat sorting in, with amused logic.

The Beauty Show.

Hundreds and Hundreds of them gathered there,
From Natural habitat out for show.
Twisting in curves and lined within each row,
Completing the portrait of dreaming stare.
Few in front displaying while some in rear.
Striving their utmost to please all in flow.
Minor grin some had, some widely they drove,
Aiming to hold on to the youth they wore.
Flowers they were beauties from all over.
By man's work, they were in an image stood.
Art it was nature bringing out nature.
Tapping in muteness, inner character,
Since splendour of those types are vision's food,
All left with their own Heart thrived to nurture.

Moonlight Memory.

Whole avenue swimming in the glitter.
Shouts of children there racing up and down.
Nightfall being jolly in that small town,
Full beaming moon was solo Spectator.
Planet mind as the only dictator,
That muddy set topping all trendy lawn,
Pains ducking beneath plans of merry crown,
My times were spent in the native flutter.
Moon sends rays as usual now too is true,
But prior infants are visibly scarce.
Lights nearer on earth looking them to woo,
Readymade world mostly handling affairs,
Rare is that shine above all to pursue.
Still child's delight lures the time with new
wears.

The First Rain.

Like those drops turn when thrown on Torrid
plate.
Relief Surged likewise from a long-warmed
land.
Blobbed masks came gushing in to change the
state.
Cutting the regime of Sky King go bland.

First shower then began easing the ground.
The aroma of wet Earth filled the air.
All hearts sprang on that fall of intense sound.
That quick contrasting season showed its flair.
And I, at my window loving it all.
Sipping my tea, grasping its subtlety,

Admired the catchy tactic of it all.
Though probing minds have guessed here things plenty,
Man's trail instructed the path it travelled.
While I sought unseen hands that enabled.

The Wakeup Call.

On opening eyes, louder grows the buzz.
All those routine humming is then commenced.
Soaring on the flies distinct from the house,
Collecting Honey is one way to spend.
Yields day-to-day supplies pockets as well.
Joy of job largely occupying thoughts.
Hands to support are other means to tell,
Winning hearts many, deeds storing wallets.
But the Soul stayed singing over all these.
Shaking now and then the whole existence.
Circling path of humans to that of flees,
With miracle lining all the essence.
Thoughts with Real buzz began to retune,
Faith beyond thence reshaping my immune.

An Open Heart.

It talks to me if filled full of its lines,
Stomach's in its large space, my thought series.
Tells of now events, or of bygone times.
I may know about the facts and fairies.
Quelling present away as it pronounced,
I'm to be trapped inside its fantasy.
Saddening me a while then I'm rejoiced,
The involved mind sometimes growing messy.
Sharing tales unlike mine, at times a match.
Nearby my life building on time boarded.
Its adventure lying in depth to catch,
Year-to-year value turning rewarded.
Two things have I blessed to cherish till end.
Books enlightening, Trust of such true friend.

The Yearly Budding.

Season elapsed, when they were of to sprout.
And in no time the branches were flooded.
Trees barren scenery going loaded,
Climate and the greens brought each other out.
Coming few with thin make, few springing
stout.
Meeting the intent as they are budded.
Life mounting in places unlimited,
The mind picked that photo to feel it out.
Like recurring dream, each year it comes in.
Ever befitting Nature's ornament.
Dressing in answer to beloved's call,
Like those good maidens at the peak are seen.
Live Bound as long in other's sentiment,
Divine love's wish in such feat do befall.

The Humble School.

A stream of what, at the start of journey.
Little wit of child followed the calling.
Clutching by, how, why entered the study.
The chase held issues with gains and falling.
Glamour of things around like a cyclone,
Youthful steps balanced on few Principles.
Several roads Tempting mind to Dethrone,
Tackling sense there battling the obstacles.
Experience pushing through thick and thin.
Judging percept observing all the change.
On losing mood with common loss and win,
Question of purpose outshined average.
In search of life, sensing took to vagueness.
Way in Spirit there held light and firmness.

Among That Line.

One among the lines touched the Source of self.
Staggering few times ensued its neck straight.
Its Talent immersed in the oil with faith,
Thrusting the shadow's foot back by itself.
As the light welled up, it was close to help.
Ardent threads nearby looked to penetrate.
Their wills picked up as fire of it gained weight.
Line by line burnt, night fell behind lit shelf.
Like festive lamps some call for unfeigned joy.
Blessings they count, sing of Soul and its cause.
In the process stirring immortal bliss.
Here in my queue of lines to self-employ,
Worldly light falling short of their cosmos,
Venture as such caught mind in its remiss.

The Home Coming.

I Flew far as dreams and desires to build.
Some smiled, some got wounds, rest reduced to
dust.
I went as feelings too, searching the field.
Few moved the Heart, few failed to keep the
trust.
As Intellect went as well with concepts.
Many cheering got me, but some jeered them.
Famines went across me, I saw the droughts.

As pride crept out, shaky grew inner frame.
And When courage slipped low like setting sun,
Views like chirping Birds tailed the
homecoming.
Silent night oppressed with far horizon.
Till crying mind remained, self strength slept in.
At Dark patience and hope pulling through test.
With Soul's advent new sight spread in my nest.

Those Words in Light.

Let the path be rugged, or with mountain.
Have river to sea as the way to go.
If lost in the progress before the gain,
The price of each in their turn is to know.
Hope centring mind and valour at large,
Take life in its bits with curious eyes,
Duties some at hand for days to discharge,
Dive deep in self and try hearing my voice.
Thou have not just sense, thoughts, mind and
body,
Thee are of true self from which all self came.
Meaningless sprint would turn thee nobody.
For I'm cosmic light, thee one form and name.
Once meditating life in light shimmered.
That flow out and in me, some words whispered.

Song Of The Falling leaf.

A farewell to this world I say,
Attend me now fair mates.
A dusk is falling at my stay,
My next Journey awaits.

Long hath I been serving this tree,
My tasks would be soon void.
But before my place turns me free,
Words I sing don't avoid.

I watched thy faces flinch away,
As thee my shape beheld.
I know my green beauty far lay,
Once youth I too upheld.

I too grew in pride at my peak,
I too tried to rule old.
But now opine them as times bleak,
Of Soul me none was told.

They say it's Guard of true nature,
Stays pure within purest.
Lies in every breathing creature,
In late times and latest.

Look around thee have many ways,
Many routes to tread on.
Open thy heart to love and praise,
Short is life to live on.

Let no guilt haunt thy consciousness.
Always thee serve along.
Abstain falling to viciousness,
In kindness, thee grow strong.

What thee shall give out would return,
Actions are of that kind.
Let willpower be thy best earn,
To manage roaming mind.

No anguish exceeds repentance,
Thoughtlessness hits the most.

Keep gentleness as thy defence,
Unwished mistake if taunt.

The boasting before nor after,
Speaks better than sheer deeds.
The joy in itself shall occur,
If demands breach not needs.

I share these not for pity's sake,
That fetches me no use.
My wrongs to warn and goods to take
May direct if confuse.

If risks incline thy steps onward,
Conduct them righteously.
At Hard times trusting graceful Lord,
Lead thyself cautiously.

Further with Lord, spirit and soul,
My times gone as novice.
Feel through them than without seemed full,
Great Bliss is the promise.

And farewell to this world I say,
Forgive if felt me rude.
A dusk is falling at my stay,
Accept blessings all good.

I'm the falling leaf of this branch,

Leaving thee old story.
In new life new way, I might launch.
This falls in memory.

A Goodbye.

To Waterfalls.

Small part of a mighty domain on Earth,
Like little Damsel of some king ago,
Thou were flowing merged in some youthful
mirth.
Letting thy history forego.

Letting none to guess thy true age of birth.
Since thee ever danced anew youth for
onlookers.

And among those eyes, those ears, happy heart,
I stood as one.
I stood there, stood with all my senses on.

Thou Majestic lady's hairs flown in air,
Looked such a beauty of kingdom's pride.
Being a part of peering beauty stare,
Thou in poet's rhythmic Heart abide.

Then thy silent, yet strong music rises.
It rose as the melody of thy dance.
What sublime notion rested behind thy song!
I did wonder.
I wondered about the Divine art of Maker.

He who made me has the place of thy Lord.
We are the offspring of same parentage.
But thou are a timeless glory of this land.
I'm merely a mortal come and go of an age.

Thee now sits in my words of applause.
I honour thee for engaging numerous hearts.
If man had only feelings, thee surpassed all
pulls.
But there lies Spirit.
A soul there is, an encasement of Hermit.

There comes the murmur of thy deepest verse.

Thy entertainment was ever booked for that
Supreme singer.
Image of whom pervades each universe.
The love of him is such that all Soul yearns to
surrender.

This flow, flow, flow shall go on.
Thy flowing is for the last chance.
Possibly till he begins the time's last dance.
During that number of Hearts may hear that
again,
And appeal thee.
Appeal thee to lend that pure love song for him,
as did me.

Stop not if only few into thy Gravity can look.
Don't change ways even if looking mind is
narrow.
All eyes will click thy beauty if not spirit
betook,
Every heart beating thus would get something to
borrow.

Bereft here are none of that great spirit.
Inherently all fit in that same longing.
Since ignorance to light, all have the moving,
In that awakening of all, thee might oblige
many.
By prompting them.

Thee may yet prompt many Divine insights and
be triumphant over some.

Then in the human flow from time to time,
perhaps life to life!
Mind clearly gripping thy way as the only at
some point.
Winning my inner domain, we shall live alike.
Eternal freedom would be thine and mine from
that moment.

Trying modestly in the flowing to that goal,
Flame of persistence rekindling my heart.
Baby steps putting through falls and rise in the
merging with that infinite Ocean,
I look for music within clinging to unconditional
love and mercy.
Whenever then He shall smile,
My smiles would sing as complete as thine with
his light remoulded in its shine.